FOUND!

ANGLO-SAXONS

Moira Butterfield

W

FRANKLIN WATTS

LONDON • SYDNEY

Franklin Watts
First published in Great Britain in 2018 by The Watts Publishing Group

HB ISBN 978 1 4451 5300 1
PB ISBN 978 1 4451 5301 8

Printed in China

Franklin Watts
An imprint of
Hachette Children's Group
Part of The Watts Publishing Group
Carmelite House
50 Victoria Embankment
London EC4Y 0DZ

An Hachette UK Company
www.hachette.co.uk

www.franklinwatts.co.uk

CONTENTS

Meet the Anglo-Saxons
SUTTON HOO BURIAL

Around 1,600 years ago a big change came to Britain. The Romans had ruled southern Britain for 400 years, but in 410 the Roman army left and bands of warriors invaded from Denmark, Germany and Holland. We call them the Anglo-Saxons. They took over land and set up their own kingdoms. One of their warrior leaders was given a magnificent burial in a ship, unearthed centuries later.

PLACE FOUND:
SUTTON HOO,
SUFFOLK.

When landowner Edith Pretty decided to investigate a group of mounds on her property, she called in local archaeologist Basil Brown. Edith was convinced there was treasure in the mounds, and she was proved right. In one of the mounds, Basil Brown uncovered a ship's metal rivets (bolts). Though the ship's wood had rotted away, the rivets still showed its outline. An Anglo-Saxon leader had been buried in the ship along with his treasures, including the remains of his helmet, shield and sword.

The creature shown here is a bird with sharp claws. It would once have decorated the leader's shield. It is about 14 cm long and made from gold, copper and red gems called garnets. There's a second smaller bird at the back of the big bird's head.

The warrior-leader's fine helmet was amongst the Sutton Hoo treasures. It is covered in pagan symbols. Can you see a dragon flying upwards on the front? It is meeting a snake coming over the top of the helmet.

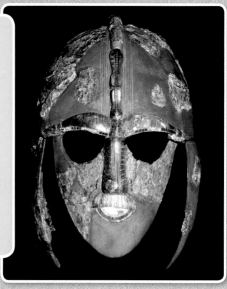

At the time of the ship burial, southern Britain was split into several kingdoms under different leaders. A tribe of people called the Angles had invaded from northern Germany and settled in East Anglia. Around 600 their leader was called King Raedwald. It may have been his grave.

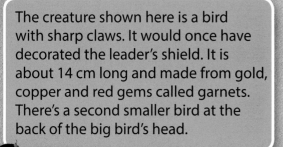

In 2016 archaeologists discovered traces of a grand wooden hall about 6 km from the Sutton Hoo burial. It might have been King Raedwald's palace, where he was based with his warriors.

When the Anglo-Saxons arrived in Britain they were pagan, which means they believed in many gods and goddesses. One of them was Odin, a powerful god of war. He had two pet ravens who pecked at the bodies of dead warriors on the battlefield. The birds on this shield probably represent those scary-sounding creatures.

The warrior-leader was buried with his finest treasures. What are the finest treasures that you own?

Grabbed in battle
STAFFORDSHIRE HOARD

In 2009 a metal detectorist discovered the biggest collection of Anglo-Saxon metal objects ever found. It had been deliberately buried, but why? And why was it mostly made up of fragments of war equipment, such as sword and helmet parts? It's possible that these were collected up from dead warriors after a battle.

Around
600-700

DATE FOUND:
2009, BY A METAL
DETECTORIST.

PLACE FOUND:
HAMMERWICH,
STAFFORDSHIRE.

The hoard was discovered under a recently ploughed field. Soon archaeologists found many more objects on the site. In all, more than 3,500 items were uncovered. There were lots of finely-made gold and silver pieces decorated with garnets, but most had been damaged or broken up before they were buried. It was actually a big pile of valuable scrap!

The oval shapes in the picture are sword guards. These sat between the sword's blade and its hilt (handle). There were lots of them in the hoard and most of them looked worn and battered, as if they had been used in battle.

Some of the pieces in the hoard were decorated with animals and red garnets. It's possible that warriors of the time thought these had magical powers to protect them in battle. Can you spot a bird beak, the head of a snake and some garnets in the treasure selection below?

The cross pictured below is a reconstruction of a crumpled-up gold cross found in the hoard (shown to the right of the reconstruction). It reveals that some Anglo-Saxons were becoming Christian at this time (see pages 8-9).

We know from Anglo-Saxon writings that warriors sometimes looted the armour and weaponry of their defeated dead enemies and buried it. It's possible the burials may have been an offering to pagan gods.

Who do you think might have buried the treasure? Perhaps you could write a story or poem about it.

Girl with a cross
TRUMPINGTON BED BURIAL

In 597 Christian monks had arrived in southeast Britain from Rome and began to convert Anglo-Saxon nobles to Christianity. The earliest Anglo-Saxon Christian grave ever found in Britain turned up on a building site in Cambridgeshire. It held a surprising secret – a bed!

Around
680

DATE FOUND:
2011, ON A BUILDING SITE.

PLACE FOUND:
TRUMPINGTON, CAMBRIDGESHIRE.

Archaeologists made the find when they were investigating a building site due to become houses. A cluster of Anglo-Saxon graves turned up, including the bed burial (shown here). A young woman aged around 16 had been laid on the bed. She was buried wearing a robe with a beautiful gold cross sewn onto the front. Bed burials are very rare, so she must have been considered a special person.

The bed was wooden, held together with iron brackets. It would have looked similar to beds made today. The wood had rotted away, but the iron brackets were still in place (you can see two of them above left).

We call items found in burials 'grave goods'. They can give us clues to who a person was and how they lived. The cross tells us that the girl was one of the first Christians in Britain. She was also buried with an iron knife, a chain that hung from her belt (for carrying things such as household tools) and glass beads that were probably decorations on a purse.

Here is the cross found in the bed burial. It was decorated with garnets. It would have been an expensive thing to own.

In early Anglo-Saxon times very little was written down, so it's impossible to get some answers, such as why Anglo-Saxon women were occasionally buried on beds. We can only make guesses based on the remains that archaeologists find.

The first British nunnery was founded in Ely, Cambridgeshire in 673, not far from this bed burial. It was set up by the daughter of the local king. Perhaps the girl in the bed was connected to the nunnery. She might even have been the daughter of an Anglo-Saxon noble who was converted to Christianity by monks.

Why do you think that some Anglo-Saxon women might have been buried in beds? Nobody knows for

Fighting the Vikings
THE YORK HELMET

In 793 a new enemy arrived to challenge the Anglo-Saxons. Viking warrior bands from Scandinavia began to take over the north and east of England, including the town of York. In 1982 a digger unearthed an Anglo-Saxon helmet in York. It may have been buried before the town fell to Vikings in 866.

Made around
775

DATE FOUND:
1982, BY A BUILDER OPERATING A DIGGER.

PLACE FOUND:
YORK, NORTH YORKSHIRE.

A mechanical digger was beginning work on a site for a new shopping centre when the digger claws struck something hard. The driver stopped to check what he had hit, and found a wood-lined pit. It contained an incredibly rare find – an Anglo-Saxon war helmet with the owner's name on it. It had been carefully stowed upside-down in the pit, perhaps for safekeeping.

On 1 November, 866, Vikings attacked York. It may have been a surprise attack while the local Anglo-Saxons were in church celebrating the Christian festival of All-Saints. The Vikings took over the town and changed its name from Eoferwic to Jorvik.

We know the York helmet was Anglo-Saxon because of the message on it. Viking helmets looked more like the reproduction helmet shown above.

Oshere, the man mentioned in the prayer, was probably the helmet's owner. He may have been a warrior who fought for a local royal family in control of York in the years before the Vikings arrived.

It's possible that the helmet might have been buried at the time of the Viking invasion of York, though we can't know for sure. Perhaps it was captured in battle, or it may have been a prized possession that was hidden from the invaders.

The iron and brass helmet had cheek pieces and a chainmail neck guard. It was decorated with animals and intertwined patterns, and it had a prayer inscribed on it in Latin. Translated, the prayer said: *In the name of our Lord Jesus Christ, the Holy Spirit and God; and to all we say amen. Oshere.*

Why do you think the helmet might have been hidden away?

A breathtaking book
LINDISFARNE GOSPELS

Anglo-Saxon monks set up monasteries around England. Here they wrote and illustrated the first books ever created in Britain.
The finest Anglo-Saxon book ever discovered, the Lindisfarne Gospels, had several lucky escapes to survive for over 1,300 years.

Early 700s

DATE FOUND: GIVEN TO THE NATION IN 1702.

PLACE FOUND: LINDISFARNE, NORTHUMBERLAND.

The book was made in the monastery of Lindisfarne but the monks who lived there fled a Viking attack in 793, taking the book with them. In 1070 monks had to hide the Gospels again, this time from Norman invaders (see page 28). In 1536 the monks finally lost the book for good when King Henry VIII closed down the monasteries in Britain. The book, already over 800 years old, was seized and kept in the Tower of London. It was eventually sold to Sir Robert Cotton, a book collector. When Cotton's collection was given to what became the British Museum, the book was finally safe.

The covers of Anglo-Saxon books were made of leather and were often beautifully decorated with gold, silver and precious jewels. The jewels were probably prized out of the Lindisfarne Gospels' cover by Henry VIII's men when they took the book in 1536.

This new cover was made for the Lindisfarne Gospels in 1852. It is based on Anglo-Saxon patterns illustrated inside the book.

The book was probably made by a monk called Eadfrith, who was the Bishop of Lindisfarne from 698 to 721. He wrote out the four gospels of the Bible in Latin. Later, lines of Old English, the language of the Anglo-Saxons, were written underneath the Latin. Eadfrith added swirling patterns around the words in a style called illumination.

Books such as this were rare and expensive in Anglo-Saxon times. They were often made for very wealthy noblemen and women, who donated money to monasteries in return. Only monks and noble families learnt how to read and write.

What is your most treasured book? Design an Anglo-Saxon book cover for it.

Life left behind
BULWORTH BOX

Ordinary Anglo-Saxon people lived in villages. They spent their days farming small strips of land. They made their own clothes and tools, and owned very little. An Anglo-Saxon cemetery found in Wiltshire has revealed some belongings from everyday life, including a box that might have been used for someone's sewing kits, or perhaps for something more magical.

600-700
Date of the cemetery

DATE FOUND:
2016, ON A BUILDING SITE

PLACE FOUND:
BULWORTH, WILTSHIRE.

The cemetery was discovered when the land was being made ready to build a housing estate. People from a local Anglo-Saxon village had been buried there with objects from their everyday lives, such as necklace beads, combs and knives. The box was found in the grave of a woman who died in her twenties.

The woman who owned the box came from one of Bulworth's farming families. They lived in houses that looked rather like sheds with thatched roofs, and spent their days looking after farm animals and crops. It was a hard life, and few people lived past their early forties at this time.

The copper box measures roughly 4 cm across and 5 cm long. It would have hung from a woman's belt, perhaps kept inside a bag. Similar boxes have been found in graves belonging to women or children around England.

The woman was buried with this cowrie shell as well as her mystery box. It comes from the Red Sea, far away from her Wiltshire home. It might have been a magical lucky charm for her, perhaps bought from a trader who visited the local area.

Boxes like this may also have held treasured lucky charms such as scraps of cloth from the robe of a holy person. There's even an idea that the boxes were used in pagan magic rituals. Perhaps more clues will turn up in the future to answer the mystery.

The box was probably buried to be useful to the woman in her afterlife. X-rays showed it had mystery scraps of metal in it, but nobody is yet sure what they are. Boxes have been found in other places with scraps of fabric, pins or plant remains inside them.

What do you think this box might have been used for?

Marvellous makers
HAMWIC PENDANT

Clues to Anglo-Saxon life have turned up all over England, sometimes in surprising places. When Southampton Football Club built a new stadium, an Anglo-Saxon cemetery was discovered under the stands! One of the finds was this gold necklace pendant, made with great skill.

Archaeologists were called in to check the building site of the new stadium. They found around 40 Anglo-Saxon graves under the area where stands are now built. The people who were buried there had their weapons and jewellery with them, perhaps to take to their afterlife. Southampton was founded back in Anglo-Saxon times. It was a port, just as it is today, but it was called Hamwic.

We don't know the names of the people buried underneath the football ground but we can guess that they were connected to the port of Hamwic. Goods were taken by boat from Hamwic to Europe, perhaps making some locals enough money to buy finely-made jewellery.

The pendant is a good example of how skilled craftspeople were in Anglo-Saxon times. It is decorated with garnets set into tiny golden sections called cells. The cells were filled with gold foil that shone through the garnets. Around the outside there are gold snakes.

Archaeologists decided to investigate only a part of the cemetery. There are thought to be more Anglo-Saxon graves under the car park and perhaps the pitch, too.

We don't know who made the Hamwic pendant but we do know of one famous Anglo-Saxon jewellery-maker, a monk called Spearhafoc. He was given the gold and jewels to make a crown for King Edward the Confessor (reigned 1042–1066). According to Anglo-Saxon writings, Spearhafoc never made the crown. Instead he ran off with the treasure!

What kind of jewellery would you design for an Anglo-Saxon?

Fashion find
PENTNEY HOARD

We know what clothes Anglo-Saxon people wore from book illustrations of the time. These pictures show us that men and women liked to decorate their clothes with brooches. Six beautiful silver Anglo-Saxon brooches were found in a Norfolk churchyard. They are now kept in London's British Museum.

DATE FOUND: 1978, BY A GRAVEDIGGER.

PLACE FOUND: PENTNEY, NORFOLK.

When church gravedigger William King stopped for a break, he noticed something metallic sticking out of the trench he had dug. He pulled out six mysterious discs and gave them to the vicar, who locked them away in a chest. Three years later a new vicar arrived, found the discs and realised they were important. We don't know why they were buried. Perhaps someone hid them to keep them safe.

The brooches are made from silver, gold and copper and are decorated with plants, animals and crosses. They were made in a style that was fashionable in late Anglo-Saxon times.

These coloured glass beads were once part of an Anglo-Saxon necklace. They were found at Cliff's End in Kent.

Anglo-Saxon men and women pinned brooches on their shoulders to hold up their clothes (buttons hadn't yet been invented).

Anglo-Saxon men pinned brooches on the cloaks they wore over wool tunics and linen undershirts. They also wore wool trousers and a belt. They were proud of their long hair and beards. Only monks and slaves had short hair.

Anglo-Saxon women wore brooches on the shoulders of the long wool tunics they wore over belted linen dresses. They also wore a veil over their long hair. They liked to wear colourful bead necklaces, too.

What clothes or jewellery do you own that you think an Anglo-Saxon person might recognise?

A history mystery
BUCKLAND CRYSTAL BALL

Early
600s

DATE FOUND:
1944, ON A
BUILDING SITE

There is still a lot we don't know about Anglo-Saxon life. One of the biggest mysteries is the purpose of the crystal balls found in the graves of some Anglo-Saxon women. What could they have been used for? This crystal ball was found in Kent.

PLACE FOUND:
BUCKLAND,
KENT.

The Buckland crystal ball was found in an Anglo-Saxon cemetery discovered when houses were being built. It belonged to a woman and it would once have hung from her belt. Most of the crystal balls found in Britain come from Kent, probably because a group of people called Jutes settled there in Anglo-Saxon times. They came from Germany and brought their customs

The ball is 25 mm wide. It is made of quartz crystal fitted inside a silver sling. Sometimes balls like this are buried with spoons that have holes in them, like tiny sieves. This ball did not have a spoon with it.

One theory is that balls of this kind were used in a magical ceremony, perhaps to heal people or to predict the future. A sieving spoon could have been used to sprinkle something in the ritual, too. Quartz pebbles have been found in some Anglo-Saxon graves, so quartz may have been seen as a magical lucky charm.

Another idea is that the balls were used to magnify delicate needlework. They could have reflected light from a candle onto the work. A third idea is that they were used to focus sunlight to light a fire.

This sieving spoon was found alongside a crystal ball in a Kent grave.

The woman who owned this crystal ball was also buried with lots of jewellery and a headband of gold thread. She was probably an important person in her community. Perhaps she perfomed magic rituals, but we'll never know for sure.

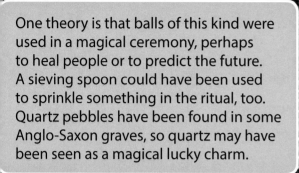

What do you think the crystal ball might have been used for?

Holy but hidden

WINCHESTER RELIQUARY

Christian Anglo-Saxons revered places and objects connected to holy saints. They made pilgrimages to see precious relics, such as the body parts of saints, kept on display in churches. The container shown here may hold a holy relic. It has a strange and mysterious story. Was it stolen and what is hidden inside it?

925-950

DATE FOUND: 1976, ON A CONSTRUCTION SITE

PLACE FOUND: WINCHESTER, HAMPSHIRE.

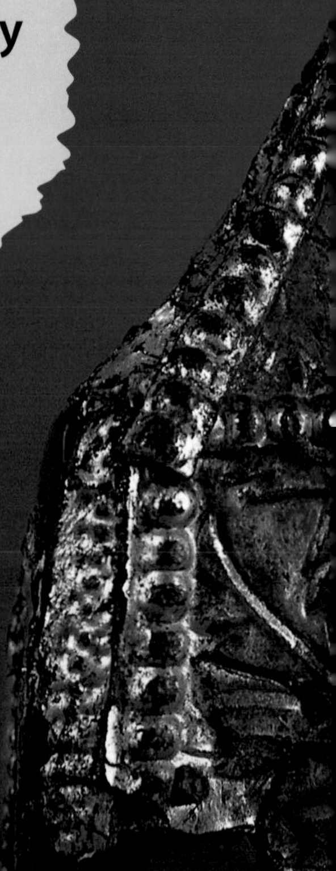

This little wooden box is called a reliquary – a container for a holy relic. It probably belonged in a church, yet it was discovered at the bottom of an Anglo-Saxon sewage pit in Winchester during preparations to build a new road. It was probably thrown in the pit around 925-950. One theory is that a thief stole it, thinking it was

The reliquary is 175 mm high and 150 mm wide. On one side there is a picture of Christ. On the other side there are pictures of leaves and flowers (shown here).

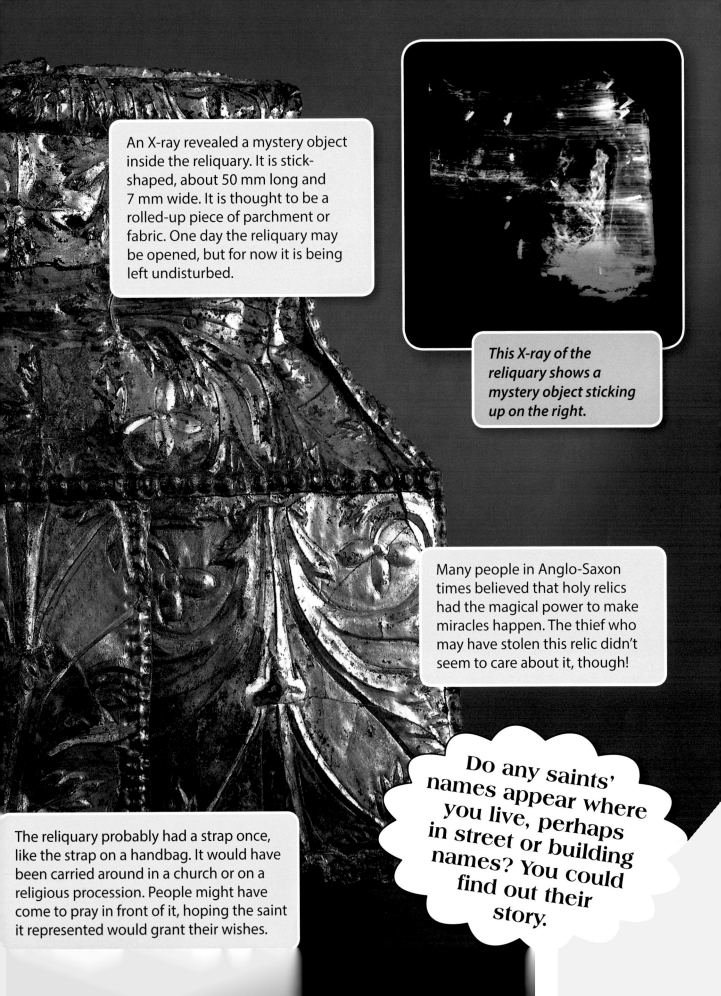

An X-ray revealed a mystery object inside the reliquary. It is stick-shaped, about 50 mm long and 7 mm wide. It is thought to be a rolled-up piece of parchment or fabric. One day the reliquary may be opened, but for now it is being left undisturbed.

This X-ray of the reliquary shows a mystery object sticking up on the right.

Many people in Anglo-Saxon times believed that holy relics had the magical power to make miracles happen. The thief who may have stolen this relic didn't seem to care about it, though!

Do any saints' names appear where you live, perhaps in street or building names? You could find out their story.

The reliquary probably had a strap once, like the strap on a handbag. It would have been carried around in a church or on a religious procession. People might have come to pray in front of it, hoping the saint it represented would grant their wishes.

Alfred the hero
ALFRED JEWEL

Between 871 and 899, King Alfred was the leader of the Anglo-Saxon kingdom of Wessex, which stretched across southern and western England. During that time he battled to save his kingdom from the Vikings and became a famous hero of English history. This beautiful find, known as the Alfred Jewel, has his name on it.

Late
800s

DATE FOUND:
1693, IN A NEWLY PLOUGHED FIELD.

PLACE FOUND:
NORTH PETHERTON, SOMERSET.

The Alfred Jewel was spotted in a newly ploughed Somerset field. It was found near the village of Athelney, where Alfred had a monastery built. It's thought to be the top of an aestel, a long pointing stick used to help read large books such as the Bible. Alfred was a learned man who encouraged people to read and write. He had several aestels made and sent to monasteries around his kingdom.

...e jewel is a small enamel (coloured glass) picture ...hind a piece of clear quartz crystal, surrounded with ...ld. Around the outside of the gold there is a message ...Old English. It says AELFRED MEC HEHT GEWYRCAN. ...modern English this means: *Alfred ordered me ...be made.*

The city of Winchester was Alfred's Wessex capital. This statue of Alfred was erected in the town in the 1800s, to celebrate him.

Alfred nearly lost his kingdom to the Vikings when they defeated him in battle in 878. He escaped and went into hiding for a while, but he returned to defeat his enemies. If Alfred had lost, the whole of England would have fallen to the Vikings.

Three other aestel tips similar to the Alfred Jewel have been found in Alfred's old kingdom of Wessex. One was found when a road was being levelled. Another was discovered by a metal detectorist and a third was found after a cliff landslide. Who knows? There might be other valuable aestels waiting to be discovered around Wessex!

How would you decorate an aestel?

Buried pennies
LENBOROUGH HOARD

King Alfred's grandson Athelstan became the first king of all of England in 927, but conflict with the Vikings wasn't over. When thousands of silver Anglo-Saxon pennies were discovered buried in a field, some of the coins showed an Anglo-Saxon ruler but others showed a Viking ruler. Why? Because it was an unusual time in English history!

Early
1000s

DATE FOUND:
2014, BY A
DETECTORIST

PLACE FOUND:
LENBOROUGH,
BUCKINGHAMSHIRE.

Metal detectorist Paul Coleman thought he had found an old bucket in a field, but then he saw some coins glinting. He had unearthed over 5,000 silver Anglo-Saxon pennies wrapped in a sheet of lead. We know roughly when they were hidden from the dates on the coins, but we don't know who hid them or why. Perhaps they intended to come back later to get them, but they never did.

Some of the coins show the head of King Ethelred the Unready. He was ruling England in 980 when Danish Vikings arrived to threaten his kingdom. At first he tried to buy them off, but eventually he had to flee for his life.

Some of the coins show the head of King Cnut. He was a Danish Viking, and he took over from Ethelred as king of England. He ruled Norway and Denmark, too. For a short time in its history, the whole of England was ruled by a Viking and was part of Scandinavia.

This coin shows the head of King Cnut, the Danish Viking who ruled England between 1016 and 1035.

By this time many Vikings had converted to Christianity. Look for a Christian cross marked on one side of the coins.

Anyone caught making fake coins in Anglo-Saxon times was condemned to death! It was seen as being a serious crime against the king himself, because the money was minted (made) by his order.

What pictures can you find on modern coins? What do they have in common with Anglo-Saxon coins?

The final battle
BAYEUX TAPESTRY

Anglo-Saxon rule came to an end in 1066. Harold, the last Anglo-Saxon king of England, was defeated by William, Duke of Normandy, at the Battle of Hastings. William's coronation began the era we call Norman times in English history. The events of the battle were illustrated on a giant embroidered roll of linen called the Bayeux Tapestry.

1070s

DATE FOUND: REDISCOVERED IN THE LATE 1700s.

PLACE FOUND: BAYEUX, NORMANDY, FRANCE.

UNITED KINGDOM

FRANCE

The Bayeux Tapestry was forgotten and nearly destroyed during its 900 years of life. After it was made it was kept at Bayeux Cathedral in France. During the French Revolution (1789-1799), it was almost used as scrap fabric to cover a wagon. Luckily a local man rescued it just in time. Later it narrowly escaped being seized and taken to Germany during the Second World War (1939-1945). Now it is back on display at Bayeux.

The 70-metre-long tapestry was probably embroidered by English women, who were famous around Europe for their embroidery skills. It may have been made on the orders of Bishop Odo of Bayeux, the half-brother of the victorious Duke William.

The embroidered story is biased towards the Normans. It tells how King Harold stole the throne of England when it should have gone by rights to William. Harold's Anglo-Saxon supporters thought differently but they lost, so they didn't get to tell their version of the story.

The tapestry artists showed some of the Normans fighting on horseback, whereas the Anglo-Saxons always fought on foot.

Harold was killed during the Battle of Hastings, and William was then crowned king. He shared out land amongst his French followers, and Anglo-Saxon leaders lost out. Many were killed or exiled. King William got rid of Anglo-Saxon laws and ran the country differently. His family ruled England for nearly a century.

Can you draw a picture similar to the Bayeux Tapestry, showing a king and his warriors in Anglo-Saxon times?

Glossary

aestel A long pointer used to help someone read a large book.

afterlife Another life that some people believes begins after a death.

Anglo-Saxons Invaders from Denmark, Holland and Germany who began settling in southern Britain around 1,600 years ago.

archaeologist Someone who digs up remains to learn more about the past.

exile To make someone leave their country

garnet A red gemstone used in Anglo-Saxon jewellery and weapon decoration.

hoard A hidden collection of treasure.

illumination A style of book decoration using illustrated borders made with patterns and tiny pictures.

Latin The language of the ancient Romans, sometimes used in Anglo-Saxon writing.

Mercia An Anglo-Saxon kingdom in central England.

metal detectorist Someone who hunts for metal underground, using an electronic metal detector.

monk A man living in a religious community called a monastery, dedicating his life to religion.

nunnery A religious community where women called nuns live, dedicating their lives to religion.

Odin A pagan god of war in Scandinavia and northern Europe.

Old English The language of the Anglo-Saxons.

pagan Someone who believes in many gods and goddesses, not the one God found in religious books such as the Holy Bible.

parchment Animal skin that has been soaked, stretched and scraped to make a thin, flat writing surface.

pilgrimage A journey to a holy place.

quartz A crystal found in rocks. It was used to decorate Anglo-Saxon jewellery. It may have been considered a lucky charm

relic Remains of something. A holy relic is an object that people think is connected to a holy person or place.

reliquary A container made for a holy relic.

ritual A ceremony that is always performed the same way.

tapestry A picture made from coloured threads sewn onto a fabric background.

Vikings Tribes from Scandinavia. Viking warriors began invading Britain in the 700s and Viking families settled in some parts of the country.

Wessex An Anglo-Saxon kingdom that stretched across south and west England.

Further Information

WEBLINKS

http://www.bl.uk/collection-items/lindisfarne-gospels
See the Lindisfarne Gospels online

https://www.youtube.com/watch?v=LtGoBZ4D4_E
See an animation of a section of the Bayeux Tapestry.

http://nvg.org.au/documents/other/anglosaxonrecipes.pdf
Take a look at some recipes inspired by the Anglo-Saxons.

TIMELINE

410   The Roman army left Britain.

449   Invaders from Germany, Denmark and Holland began to arrive in southeast Britain. We call them the Anglo-Saxons.

597   Christian monks arrived on a mission to convert the Anglo-Saxons to Christianity.

600   Around this time King Raedwald, leader of the East Angles, may have been buried in a ship at Sutton Hoo.

Early 700s   The Lindisfarne Gospels were made.

793   The Vikings began attacking the British Isles.

866   The Vikings attacked and conquered York. They named it Jorvik.

878 Alfred, King of Wessex, defeated the Danish Vikings at the Battle of Edington. The Danes and the Anglo-Saxons agreed to split England between them.

927   Alfred's grandson Athelstan defeated the Vikings and ruled over the whole of England.

1016   Danish King Cnut became king of England.

1066   Harold, the last Anglo-Saxon king, was defeated at the Battle of Hastings by William, Duke of Normandy.

Index